CULTURES OF THE WORLD

LATVIA

Robert Barlas

MARSHALL CAVENDISH
New York • London • Sydney

Reference edition published 2000 by
Marshall Cavendish Corporation
99 White Plains Road
Tarrytown
New York 10591

© Times Editions Pte Ltd 2000

Originated and designed by
Times Books International, an imprint of
Times Editions Pte Ltd

Printed in Malaysia

Library of Congress Cataloging-in-Publication Data:

Barlas, Robert.
    Latvia / Robert Barlas.
      p. cm.—(Cultures of the World)
    Includes bibliographical references and index.
    ISBN 0-7614-0977-7 (library binding)
    1. Latvia—Juvenile literature. I. Title. II. Series.
DK504.56.B37   2000
947.96—dc21   99–30168
                CIP
                AC

INTRODUCTION

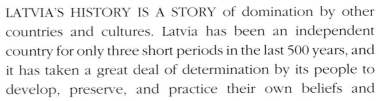

LATVIA'S HISTORY IS A STORY of domination by other countries and cultures. Latvia has been an independent country for only three short periods in the last 500 years, and it has taken a great deal of determination by its people to develop, preserve, and practice their own beliefs and traditions. The most recent occupation, that of the Soviet Union, lasted for 50 years and almost destroyed the physical infrastructure of the country.

Latvia still has a great deal to overcome and a lot of problems to solve, but the spirit of its people is strong, and their history indicates that they are not easily beaten. As the influence of the former Soviet Union is erased, Latvia will once again take its rightful place as a productive and influential northern European country and its cultural traditions will strengthen again as they have in the past.

CONTENTS

Art is an important part of Latvian culture. This wooden construction is one of many pieces of modern sculpture displayed around the country.

CONTENTS

Latvian children of today are born into a productive nation, despite the years of foreign domination.

GEOGRAPHY

LATVIA IS LOCATED IN NORTHERN EUROPE. The country covers an area of 25,400 square miles (65,786 square km), which is roughly equal in size to West Virginia, or to the combined territories of Belgium and the Netherlands in Europe. Latvia lies across the Baltic Sea from Sweden, south of Finland and Estonia, north of Lithuania and Belarus, and west of Russia. Its western boundary runs along the shores of the Baltic Sea and the Gulf of Riga.

Latvia is situated on the northern edge of the European Plain, a relatively flat landscape with gently rolling hills. The characteristics of the land were formed during the Ice Age when large masses of ice moved across the area. The Baltic Sea coast of Latvia consists of a coastal plain 308 miles (496 km) long. The flatness of this area, a former sea bottom, is occasionally broken by coastal ridges, but plains are the predominant land form throughout the country.

Opposite: **Harvest time on a farm outside Riga.**

Left: **A Latvian fishing in the flood plain of a river after heavy rains.**

Long stretches of sandy beach line Latvia's Baltic Sea coast.

REGIONS

Latvia is divided into five major regions—Zemgale, Kurzeme, Vidzeme, Latgale, and the capital area of Riga.

The region of Zemgale is bisected by the Zemgale Plain, and is dominated by the river Lielupe. The plain is a depository of sandy clay and is the most fertile grain-producing area of the country. Hilly areas can be found to the west and in the southeast part of the region, especially at its borders with the Daugava, Latvia's principal river.

To the west, the region of Kurzeme is more undulating than that of Zemgale, while Vidzeme to the northeast, and Latgale to the east are much more hilly. The hills are interspersed with lowland areas, river valleys, lakes, marshes, and boglands. The soil of Vidzeme and Latgale is poorer and less suited to crop farming than in Zemgale and Kurzeme. Latgale is crisscrossed by streams and interconnected by lakes with numerous islets, and it is often referred to as Latvia's lake district.

LATVIA

Feet		Meters
16,500		5,000
9,900		3,000
6,600		2,000
3,300		1,000
1,650		500
660		200
0		0

N

0   25   50   75 Miles

0   25   50   75   100 Kilometers

Rivers and lakes play an important role in the cultural and national identity of the Latvians. They are the subject of many Latvian legends and folk songs, which refer to their origins and beauty and to events that occurred on them.

LAKES AND MOUNTAINS

Latvia is a very low country. The average elevation is only 292 feet (89 m) above sea level, while its highest point, called Gaizins, located in the uplands of central Vidzeme, is only 1,017 feet (310 m).

There are almost 3,000 lakes in Latvia. The largest is Lake Rezna covering an area of 21 square miles (54 square km). The deepest is Lake Dridzis at 215 feet (65 m). Both lakes are located in the Latgale region in the east.

RIVERS

The four major rivers in Latvia are the Daugava, Lielupe, Venta, and Gauja, but there are numerous small rivers, some 1,000 in all.

The Daugava, which begins in central Russia, is the largest river, flowing through Latvia to the Gulf of Riga. According to legend, it was dug out by animals and birds, and many of its islands were created by the devil in his attempts to block the river's flow.

The Venta originates in Lithuania. It is renowned for its waterfall, called the Rumba, at the city of Kuldiga. The river mouth forms a natural harbor for oceangoing ships at Ventspils, where it flows into the Baltic Sea.

A view of the Daugava as it flows into the Gulf of Riga.

CLIMATE AND SEASONS

Despite being situated quite far north, Latvia's climate is relatively temperate, with mild winters and moderately warm summers. Spring comes in late March when flooding is common, due to melting snow and the break-up of river ice. The mild, warm summer weather arrives in June and lasts until September. This is the season of the heaviest rainfall, with frequent thunderstorms and hail. Typically, July is the warmest month of the year, with an average temperature of 64°F (18°C).

During the autumn months, there is frost, high humidity, and fog, particularly in coastal areas. Winter sets in around November. January is the coldest month, with an average temperature of 23°F (-5°C). Most snowfall occurs between January and March. Despite the small size of the country, there are marked differences in climate from west to east in Latvia.

While the ports on the coast of Kurzeme remain ice-free in winter, the Gulf of Riga and the mouth of the Daugava freeze over.

FLORA AND FAUNA

There are three main plant habitats in Latvia—coniferous and broadleaf forests, swampy marshes, and grass-covered meadows. Forests cover approximately 26% of the country.

In Latvia there are about 13,000 kinds of animals. Around 60 species of mammals are known, including rodents, such as squirrels and beavers, and carnivores such as the wolf, fox, lynx, and marten. Many of Latvia's animals can also be found in other countries in the region—wild boar, elk, red deer, and the swamp turtle.

The American mink and the Norwegian rat have been accidentally introduced into Latvia. Other non-native animals are the jenot (a kind of raccoon), fallow deer, and wild rabbits.

There are over 300 species of birds in Latvia, of which about 50 inhabit the country all year round. These include the common water fowl, turtle and rock doves, several species of grouse, the barn owl, the house swallow, the greenish warbler, and even the Arctic loon.

MAJOR CITIES

Most of Latvia's present-day urban centers evolved from early settlements near rivers and other sites along trade routes. The cities developed their own local traditions, religious character, and political systems, which were tempered over the years by the various occupying powers—the Poles, Swedes, Germans, and Russians. The major cities in Latvia today are Riga, Daugavpils, Liepaja, Jelgava, Jurmala, and Ventspils.

RIGA Riga is the capital of Latvia. It is situated on the Daugava River estuary where it flows into the Baltic Sea.

Riga was founded by the German Knights of the Sword who built fortresses along the river. The Citadel of Riga was built in the 17th century, and Riga soon became one of the strongest fortresses on the eastern coast of the Baltic Sea.

During the 1930s, Riga was referred to as "the Paris of the north" with its grand streets and broad boulevards. The old historic part of the city, known as the Old Town (or *Vecriga*), has been preserved and protected over the centuries, and most of the area has been restored to its original state with narrow cobblestone streets, richly decorated doors, tile roofs, and churches.

The focal point of the modern city of Riga is the Liberty Monument, where Latvians gather to show their love and devotion to their homeland and to remember the despair and hope of the long years of the Soviet occupation.

A view over the Old Town of Riga from St. Peter's Church toward the docks on the Baltic coast.

13

DAUGAVPILS Daugavpils, the second largest city in Latvia, is situated in the southeast on the Daugava River. The first written record of Daugavpils is from 1275, but archaeological digs show that the area has been inhabited since the Stone Age. Daugavpils is the administrative center of the Latgale region and is an important transportation junction in eastern Latvia. Due to its proximity to Russia, Belarus, and Lithuania, Daugavpils has become an important center of trade and commerce.

Daugavpils is also noted for its rich and varied cultural activity. There are some 15 national cultural institutions supporting their own cultures, while the Daugavpils Pedagogical University is noted as a national training center for teachers.

Many of the buildings in the old sections of Latvian cities have been restored to their former glory following independence.

LIEPAJA

LIEPAJA Liepaja is located on Lake Liepaja where its waters enter the Baltic Sea. It has a population of 98,000 and has been inhabited since the ninth century. Liepaja has been part of many different countries since 1625, including Sweden, Prussia, and the former Soviet Union.

One of the city's major features is its artificial harbor, which was built between 1697 and 1703. It was deepened in the middle of the 19th century to remain ice-free during the cold winter months. As a gateway to the West the entry became an important communications center in 1869 when it was linked with Copenhagen by an undersea cable.

During the Soviet occupation, access to Liepaja was restricted because of the large Russian naval base there. Today, Liepaja is noted for its excellent port facilities, as well as being an important Latvian industrial center.

Liepaja's port facilities include large dry-dock facilities for ship repair.

JELGAVA Jelgava is situated on the banks of the Lielupe river, which serves as a major transportation route between Riga and Lithuania. It was officially founded in 1573 but was mentioned in historic documents dating back to 1265.

As the capital of the Zemgale region, Jelgava first developed as an active trade and commerce center. During the 18th century it was also a printing center. The first Latvian newspaper, *Latviesu Avizes*, was printed there as were half of all Latvian language books. Today, industrial activity in Jelgava includes textile mills, agricultural machinery plants, and a sugar refinery.

Jelgava's most important landmark is the 300-room, Baroque-style Jelgava Castle, which was designed by the Italian architect F. B. Rastrelli. It took over 30 years to complete. It is located on the site of a castle built by the Livonian Order in 1265, near the Lielupe River. The original castle was destroyed during World War I, but it was rebuilt during Latvia's first period of independence.

VENTSPILS Ventspils is located on the shores of the Baltic Sea at the mouth of the Venta River in western Latvia. The city was an important trade and commercial center throughout its history, and the mouth of the Venta was known to navigators as early as the 12th century. In early times it was inhabited by the Vend tribes, then by the Livonian Order in the 13th century.

Ventspils became a major shipbuilding center, producing ships for England, France, and Italy. During the 17th century it was the headquarters of the Duchy of Courland, which included Kurzeme and Zemgale provinces.

The city continues to be a major transportation center. The main activity of the port is transshipment of oil and petroleum products, and the city has a number of gas and oil refineries and chemical manufacturing facilities. Today, major ecological clean-up efforts are underway in Ventspils to begin to repair the damage caused from extensive environmental neglect during the Soviet era.

Ventspils was founded in 1242 and is known for its ice-free port.

HISTORY

THE FIRST INHABITANTS OF LATVIA were nomadic tribes who migrated along the Baltic Sea after the last Ice Age some 10,000 years ago. By 2000 B.C., a new group of settlers came from the south and established permanent settlements in Latvia, Lithuania, and East Prussia.

These Baltic tribes—Cours, Semigallians, Livs, Sels, and Letgallians—lived in the area of Latvia from the second to the fifth centuries A.D. After the sixth century A.D., pressure from the Slavs in the east and the Vikings in the west forced most of the Baltic tribes to retreat north, reinforcing their settlements as they went.

The Germans were the first to succeed in invading Latvia. The first German merchants arrived in the second half of the 12th century, spurred on by the Crusades, which were beginning to focus attention on converting the non-Christian nations of Northern and Eastern Europe.

Opposite: **An aerial view of the magnificent Liberty Monument in Riga, built to celebrate freedom from Russian control.**

Left: **Between the second and fifth centuries A.D., Baltic tribes traded the semiprecious stone, amber, and the link between the Baltic countries and those on the Mediterranean Sea became known as the Amber Route.**

19

THE DUCHY OF COURLAND

By the end of the 13th century, the Latvians, including tribes in what is now known as Estonia, were under complete German domination, and the area was united into a state known as the Confederation of Livonia. For the next 270 years, Latvians lived under German rule.

German rule came to an end during the Livonian War of 1558–1582 with the invasion of Latvia by Ivan the Terrible of Russia. The Russians were not completely successful in conquering Livonia, as they faced opposition from the Poles. As a result, the greater part of Latvia eventually fell to the Kingdom of Poland, while the western part of Latvia became the Duchy of Courland. For the next 200 years, the Duchy of Courland remained an independent naval and commercial power in Northern Europe with its own army, navy, and until 1795, its own monetary system.

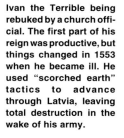

Ivan the Terrible being rebuked by a church official. The first part of his reign was productive, but things changed in 1553 when he became ill. He used "scorched earth" tactics to advance through Latvia, leaving total destruction in the wake of his army.

FOREIGN DOMINATION

The economic and social domination of the Latvian people reached its lowest point during Polish and Russian domination. Landlords acquired more and more land and forced excessive demands on the peasants.

Latvia continued to be a political football for many years. During the Polish-Swedish war of 1600 to 1629, Sweden acquired the region of Vidzeme. The Swedish king, Gustav II, brought about immediate administrative and judicial reforms, and made great efforts to strengthen Lutheranism and foster education. The Swedes ruled Vidzeme until 1710.

During the Great Northern War from 1710 to 1795, the Russians began conquering parts of Latvia once again, until the whole country was under Russian control. The Swedish judicial reforms were thrown out and the conditions of Latvian peasants deteriorated once more. Their compulsory labor was increased to six days a week, while the landed gentry were exempt from taxation. To support their lavish lifestyle landlords demanded higher taxes from the peasants.

The demands made of the Latvian peasants during Russian domination forced them further into debt. Farmers in Latvia are still poor and use traditional machinery on the land.

NATIONAL AWAKENING BEGINS

The Age of Enlightenment, a period when a belief developed in the power of reason, science, and the possibility of human change for the better, spread through Europe in the 18th century, but was slow in coming to Latvia. Although a tract advocating the complete emancipation of the peasants was published early in the 19th century, the German-born gentry strongly opposed any reforms and were powerful enough to resist change for a long time. Finally, a series of laws were passed in which the peasants were given personal freedom and limited freedom of movement. However, they were still dependent on their landlords for their livelihood. A major breakthrough came in 1868 when a law was passed eliminating mandatory service to manors. This forced the gentry to hire labor and to sell an ever increasing amount of land to their former tenants to obtain cash.

The most promient leaders of the first National Awakening Movement, which began in 1856, were writers—Krisjanis Barons, Krisjanis Valdemars, Juris Alunans, and later Atis Kronvalds—all of whom were known for their patriotism.

During the Age of Enlightenment, trade through Riga expanded.

RUSSIFICATION

As a result of finally being able to buy their own land, a much larger number of Latvians became landowners in the latter part of the 19th century and so began to have the financial resources to educate their children and take part in social and cultural activities. With this growth of education, Latvians became reacquainted with their past history and with their ethnic heritage, which led in turn to a growth in national identity.

Ironically, at the same time as this reawakening of national feeling, Latvia was undergoing a major wave of Russification—Russians only in all official positions, the Russian language mandatory in schools and in all institutions, and enforcement of the Russian Orthodox faith. The revolution of 1905 in Russia was a turning point which inspired the Latvians to take up arms against their German landlords and Russian rulers. Although this revolt was put down mercilessly by Czarist troops, the stage was set for Latvia's war of independence 13 years later.

This map in a Riga public building shows the distances between Riga to important cities in the Soviet Union. The place names are written in Russian and Latin scripts.

Above: **Officers of the Latvian army being addressed by Prime Minister Karlis Ulmanis after they defeated the Bolsheviks and secured independence.**

Opposite: **The Monument for Liberators in Jelgava bears testament to the struggle Latvia has endured during its long fight for independence.**

INDEPENDENCE

On November 18, 1918, Latvians declared national independence and formed a provisional government. The war of independence had begun. Fighting continued for the next two years against the Bolsheviks in Russia, who despite Lenin's promises, wanted to incorporate Latvia into the new Soviet Union, and also against the Germans, who had similar plans for Latvia.

The Germans and the Bolsheviks were both defeated by 1920. Latvia signed a peace treaty with the Soviet Union wherein it recognized "unconditionally the independence and sovereignty of Latvia and declines, voluntary and for all times, all claims on the Latvian people and territory which formerly belonged to Russia." Latvia was established as a democratic republic, and the first period of Latvia's real political independence began.

Latvia's democratic, parliamentary government was recognized by all the world powers and Latvia joined the League of Nations in 1922.

A NEW ECONOMY

Following independence, laws were passed concerning the redistribution of land, and the number of landowning farmers increased by nearly 100%. The first decade of independence also saw the rebuilding of the economy. New industries were built around natural resources, while the State Electrotechnical Factory began to produce radios and telephone equipment. A hydroelectric generating station supplied 40% of Latvia's electric power.

MOLOTOV-RIBBENTROP PACT

But Latvia's independence did not last. In 1939 the Soviet Union and Nazi Germany signed the Molotov-Ribbentrop Pact, which included a secret protocol that consigned independent Latvia to the Soviet sphere of influence.

In 1940 Latvia received an ultimatum from Moscow demanding the immediate free entry of Soviet troops into Latvia's territory. The Red Army occupied Latvia the following day, and a Soviet-installed government took power. During the next 12 months, over 32,000 people were deported or executed, and entire families were sent to labor camps in Siberia.

VIENOTI LATVIJAI

This striking monument in Latgale commemorates the freedom fighters' struggle to escape foreign domination.

SOVIET LATVIA

In 1941 the German Nazis occupied the country, exacting their own terror on the populace. Initially, Latvians hoped that the Germans would reinstate Latvia's independence, but this did not happen, and in 1944 Latvia was once again reoccupied by the Soviet Union.

This time, Russian dominance was to last for nearly 50 years and bring with it new waves of terror and deportations. Armed resistance against the Russian occupation lasted until 1952 when it was finally crushed and all symbols of Latvia's independence were outlawed or altered. Russian was imposed as the official language, farms were collectivized and industry nationalized, a large number of Russians were relocated to Latvia, and most personal liberties were suppressed.

For the next 50 years, the seat of government and the real power was in Moscow, and Latvia was subjected to a totalitarian way of life. Private ownership was prohibited and intellectual work was devalued. The state controlled every aspect of an individual's life—from cradle to grave.

Children attended state-run kindergartens, then entered state-run schools. In their teens they had to join the Young Pioneers—a state-run organization for young people where control could be maintained over the activities of members and where ongoing political and social indoctrination could be conducted.

COLLECTIVE FARMS

With private property abolished, most city inhabitants were forced to live in apartments that belonged to the state. They tended to be small and cramped and not ideal places to bring up a family. The rent was set at a fixed rate, but the government had the power to raise it at their will.

In the countryside, family farms were liquidated and replaced by state-controlled collective farms. Pride in work and in one's surroundings disappeared as personal freedom of movement was curtailed. Civil liberties ceased to exist, and arrests, interrogations, and deportations were common.

Today, in some parts of independent Latvia, collective farms have been disbanded in favor of smaller, family-run agricultural businesses.

ISOLATION FROM THE WEST

By the 1960s, the Iron Curtain was absolute—no communications existed with the West and news from other parts of the world was not available, except when it suited the government.

Until the early 1980s, most people in Latvia had never seen a picture of a Western world leader, such as the prime minister of Britain or the American president. The desire of the populace to regain independence was silenced by the state rule of the Communist Party and the KGB, and religious and human rights activists were routinely arrested and consigned to prison camps in the Soviet Union.

Until the late 1980s, the campaign for Latvia's independence in the international political arena could only be carried on by the over 120,000 Latvian exiles in the West who had fled the country in 1944 and 1945.

LATVIA TODAY

Latvia's third National Awakening began with a demonstration in 1987 in defiance of local authorities. It was held at the Liberty Monument in Riga to commemorate the victims of the 1941 Soviet deportation. After this, with each subsequent rally and demonstration, the old rules established by the Soviet regime began to fall. Latvian was declared the official language of the republic, and the national flag was reinstated after a mammoth demonstration of 300,000 people in July 1988. In 1989 the largest ever Baltic demonstration—the "Baltic Way"— was held. A 400-mile (644-km) long human chain, made up of an estimated 2 million people, was formed that stretched from Tallinn in Estonia, through Riga to Vilnius in Lithuania.

On May 4, 1990, after the collapse of a coup in Moscow, the provisional Latvian parliament voted to restore Latvia's prewar status as an independent republic. In 1993 the first free parliamentary elections were held, and the prewar currency, the Latvian lat, again became the official currency. In 1994 Latvian president Guntis Ulmanis and his Russian counterpart, Boris Yeltsin, signed an agreement to withdraw all Russian troops from Latvian soil. In 1995 Latvia became an independent member of the Council of Europe.

Today, Latvia is once again a country in its own right, and although it will take a long time to recover from many centuries of foreign domination and the complete ruination of the economy, Latvians are working hard to do just this as soon as they can.

Boris Yeltsin was the Russian leader in power when Russia agreed to remove all its troops from Latvia.

GOVERNMENT

LATVIA IS AN INDEPENDENT DEMOCRATIC REPUBLIC. The constitution provides for separation of legislative, executive, and judicial powers; for the separation of church and state; for freedom of the press, conscience, speech, and assembly; and for equal rights for all citizens, including cultural autonomy for ethnic minorities.

The major political parties in the *Saeima*, or parliament, include the Democratic Party, *Saimnieks*, with 21 deputies who advocate stronger ties to Moscow and more centralized control by the state; the Alliance Party, *Latvijas cels*, with 16 deputies, which is a coalition of unified centrists and pronationalists who strongly advocate a free-market economy; and the *Tevzeme un Briviba* party with 14 deputies who want strong measures to protect the Latvian culture and language. There are currently 15 deputies sitting in parliament as independents.

Opposite: **Before Latvian independence, an assorted mix of ethnic Latvians, Estonians, Ukranians and Lithuanians showed their support for the democratic freedom of the Baltic people from Soviet control.**

Left: **The somber parliament building in Riga houses the *Saeima*.**

NATIONAL AND LEGAL STRUCTURES

Ultimate power is vested in a single-chamber parliament, the *Saeima*, which has 100 elected deputies whose term is three years. The deputies have control over domestic legislation and international treaties, determine the size of the armed forces, and have veto power over the national budget, which is proposed by the cabinet.

The president is elected by the *Saeima* for a term of five years for a maximum of two consecutive terms. The president can initiate legislation, appoint diplomatic representatives, and is the commander-in-chief of the armed forces. He has the power to initiate the dissolution of the *Saeima*, but the *Saeima* has the power to dismiss the president by a two-thirds vote.

The president appoints the prime minister, who has the power to choose the members of the cabinet, consisting of 12 ministers and four state ministers, who have voting rights on matters in their areas of responsibility.

The judicial structure consists of township courts, justices of the peace, juvenile courts, district courts, a court of appeals, and the supreme court.

CURRENT POLITICAL ISSUES

The current government's policy is to move Latvia away from Russian influence, entrenched during the Soviet occupation, and realign with Europe as was the case before the Russians came. There is still visible evidence of the long Soviet occupation on the streets of Riga.

The government is active in making preparations for Latvia to become a member of the European Union (EU) and a member of NATO, although there is some resistance in the country to this direction. Improving the economic health of the country by attracting foreign capital and investment to Latvia is also an important agenda item for the current government.

Opposite: **Guntars Krasts was prime minister until 1998. He was one of Latvia's first entrepreneurs after the Russians were overthrown and owned several real estate companies before he became the minister of economics in 1995.**

Below: **The defensive wall around the parliament buildings in Riga still bears the marks of the days when the Red Army patrolled the streets.**

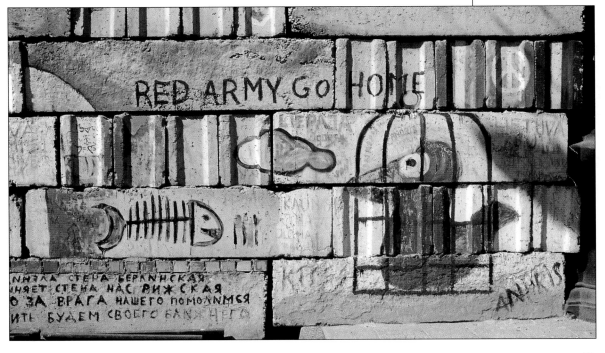

IMMIGRANTS

The issue of acquiring Latvian citizenship through naturalization for foreigners is one of the most difficult matters for the government. The largest group of "noncitizens" consists of Russians (63% of all noncitizens), followed by Belorussians (12%), and Ukranians (8%). The Latvian government wants to ensure that Latvia maintains its identity as a country but also offers citizenship to the various non-Latvian groups that reside there. As a result, top priority is now placed on promoting social integration and ensuring that the naturalization of persons willing to become citizens of Latvia takes place with speed and efficiency.

Members of the immigrant population can be found in all areas of society, including the armed forces and government.

RECENT ELECTIONS

Participation in the political process by the Latvian people has declined since the euphoric first years after independence, as a certain level of cynicism has developed. There are many political parties and no clear distinction among them. Thus, in the general election in 1995, there was no clear winner, and a coalition government had to be formed by many different parties.

In the last election more women voted than men, and residents of rural areas and small towns were more likely to vote than inhabitants of Riga, perhaps due to the fact that a greater proportion of noncitizens live in the capital.

Public impatience for the economic and social benefits of reform is rising, but official corruption is not yet under complete control. The assumption still prevails that some government officials—particularly the bureaucrats—operate as if they were still under the communist regime, thus fostering distrust.

There are still issues the Latvian people are not satisfied with in the new structure of the country, and demonstrations on local and national issues take place throughout the country.

LATVIA'S CURRENT LEADERS

Guntis Ulmanis, president of Latvia in 1999, was born in 1939 to a very famous political family—his great uncle, Karlis Ulmanis, was the last president of independent Latvia before it was invaded in World War II.

Very early in his life, his whole family was deported by the Russians to Siberia. Following their return in 1946, Ulmanis graduated with a degree in economics and was drafted by the Soviet army, as all young Latvian men then were. He became a member of the Communist Party in 1965, but resigned in 1969. After first working as a university lecturer, and then at a number of jobs in the public service, he was elected to the Latvian parliament in 1993 and became president in the same year.

Latvia's president, Guntis Ulmanis, at a demonstration for children's rights.

THE ROLE OF THE MILITARY

Currently, the national forces of Latvia include the Ministry of Defense, the Home Guard, the Ministry of Internal Affairs, and the Security Service.

The armed forces of the Ministry of Defense include a reconnaissance battalion, a mobile infantry battalion, an engineering battalion, and the Air Defense Force. Men between the ages of 19 and 27 may be conscripted for a one-year tour of duty in the army. Its main roles today are the defense of the country's borders and peacekeeping missions outside of the country.

Military units are responsible for guarding prisons and other places of confinement, and two battalions of mobile police come under the authority of the Ministry of Internal Affairs to assist customs officials at border points.

The Home Guard is under the direct authority of the president. The Security Service consists of a special battalion of soldiers whose job it is to fight against terrorists and to provide escorts for visiting dignitaries.

The Latvian Navy's Frontier Guard, whose ships hold strong positions in Latvia's numerous ports.

ECONOMY

WITH INDEPENDENCE REGAINED at the beginning of the 1990s, Latvia inherited the remnants of the state-controlled industries that had been under Moscow's control for 50 years. The new leaders had the difficult task of moving the country from a centralized, state-controlled economy to a free-market-style economy.

Major industries, which had been totally dependent on raw materials and energy from the former Soviet Union, are now being privatized, upgraded, and restructured to become competitive with those in Western economies. Most businesses targeted for privatization can be leased, with an option to buy, to any Latvian, or they are sold outright at auction.

By 1996, more than 93% of state-owned enterprises had been privatized through the Latvian Privatization Agency. By the end of the 1990s, the private sector produced almost 90% of the country's gross domestic product (GDP).

Opposite: **The manufacture of food products, such as smoked fish, is one of Latvia's largest primary industries.**

Left: **The docks in Riga are a dramatic backdrop to the urban skyline. The busy port services the country's import and export industries.**

An operator working on the production line of a state machine-building factory. State-owned industries are being privatized in a bid to boost the country's economy.

INDUSTRIES

Latvia's major industries are food and beverage manufacturing, lumbering, construction, farming, fisheries, and transportation services.

Hydroelectric power is generated in Latvia by three hydroelectric generating stations located on the Daugava river. Approximately 50% of Latvia's electricity supply comes from Estonia, Lithuania, and Russia. Latvia has no oil or natural gas deposits, so gas is imported from Russia. Peat is still used as an energy source and is also exported.

Latvia's chief exports are lumber and agricultural products. Its main export partners are Russia, the Commonwealth of Independent States (CIS), Germany, Sweden, Great Britain, Finland, and Lithuania.

Russia and the CIS are also the largest exporters to Latvia. However, imports from European Union countries constitute the largest overall percentage and include machinery and equipment, clothing, chemical products, and vehicles.

WORKING LIFE

The employment code approved by the Latvian government in 1992 regulates all employment legislation, and a minimum wage is set by law. Every employee has a "work book" documenting their work history that must be presented when starting employment and is returned upon termination. The typical work week in industry is 40 hours in a five-day week. Vacations may range from two weeks to one month.

In the countryside, working life on single family farms is difficult because of the lack of farm machinery. The high cost of gasoline has forced many farms to return to using horses rather than tractors and other mechanized machinery, and much of the heavy work is done manually. All the work is usually done, without any hired help, by the farmer's family, who also produce most of their own food.

The average unemployment rate in Latvia is about 9%, but in some parts of the country, it is as high as 25%, particularly in the eastern region and among low-skilled workers.

A lumberjack working for a private logging company uses up-to-date machinery to work quickly and efficiently. Some small farms cannot afford to purchase modern machinery and are forced to work manually.

REVENUE AND TRADE

With the regaining of independence, Latvia had to introduce its own system of revenue generation,. Today, the main sources of revenue are taxes—mainly a social welfare tax in the form of a payroll tax.

In 1996 Latvia traded with 140 countries, exporting to 104 countries and importing from 133 countries. Latvia has established free-trade agreements with the European Free Trade Association, and the ultimate integration of Latvia into the European Union is one of the most important objectives of the government.

Negotiations are under way to establish a Baltic Customs Union, which would mean elimination of trade barriers between member states (Estonia, Latvia, and Lithuania), the free movement of capital and labor, harmonization of taxation systems, as well as a joint policy of foreign trade.

The Latvian currency, the lat, was introduced following Latvian independence.

TRANSPORTATION

As in many other parts of the world, ownership of a car is the aim of every Latvian family. As a result, the number of cars on the roads is growing at a rapid rate. The condition of highways and roads is being improved gradually, while city streets are slowly being restructured after decades of neglect during the Soviet period. In rural areas, bus transportation is most common, although in some remote places local inhabitants still rely on horses.

There are three main sea ports that can accommodate oceangoing vessels in Latvia—Ventspils, Riga, and Liepaja. The main activity in these ports is the transshipment of cargo from countries formerly part of the Soviet Union to countries in the West. There are also a number of small fishing ports dotted along the coast of the Gulf of Riga.

Riga airport is the largest airport, handling local and international passenger and cargo traffic, while Liepaja airport directs only local traffic— both passenger and cargo.

The main ports in Latvia are among the largest and busiest in the Baltic states.

LATVIANS

THE POPULATION OF LATVIA is about 2.5 million. True Latvians make up 55% of the population, while the remainder is made up of a mixture of ethnic groups. Russians and Ukranians make up 32.5%. Minority populations include Poles at 2.2%, Lithuanians, 1.3%, and Estonians, 0.1%.

After Latvia regained independence in 1991, citizenship was granted to all pre-World War II citizens and their descendants. Some 29% of the total population of Latvia are still noncitizens, the majority of whom are Russian-speaking immigrants.

Half of all Latvia's Russians live in Riga, making up the majority of the capital's inhabitants. The Latvian Russians are not a unified national community—they are a broad group split into many social classes, with differing interests and political orientation. Many Russians work in the industrial sector, with a few in agriculture. Some of the younger generation of Russians are very active in business and enterprise.

Opposite: **Latvians are very proud of their heritage, and folk dress can often be seen on festivals and holidays.**

Left: **The new generation of Latvian children is being brought up in a more stable, newly-independent country.**

ETHNIC MINORITIES

RUSSIANS Russians were the largest minority in Latvia after World War I. By 1935, there were 206,499 Russians in Latvia. By 1989, the number had increased to 905,515. Recently, in the years after Latvia regained independence, a wave of Russian emigration has begun to take place— between 1992 and 1994 some 62,000 returned to Russia.

Latvian Russians are culturally united by their use of the Russian language, rather than by their nationality. Russian intellectuals have formed a number of organizations to promote Russian culture and education in Latvia.

Despite Latvia's separation from Russia in recent years, many Russians have chosen to stay in what has become their homeland.

The Latvian Russian Cultural Center, founded in 1994, united seven Russian organizations, including the Russian Children's Choir and the Russian folk instrument orchestra. Some Russian organizations are also working in the opposite direction by introducing Latvian culture to the Russian population.

In a number of schools in Latvia the curriculum is taught in Russian, but this has begun to change since independence in Latvia. These schools are giving up the standardized Russian curriculum forced on them during the Soviet period and are concentrating on establishing an independent Russian language stream within the Latvian national educational system.

The older generation of Latvians is able to recount first-hand experiences of life in Latvia under several different foreign occupations.

UKRANIANS As of 1995, Ukranians made up 2.73% of the population of Latvia. Most of them live in the city of Liepaja and have not really integrated into Latvian society. Just under 17% of them speak Latvian, and most consider Russian as their native tongue, rather than Ukranian.

Many Ukranians in Latvia are former officers from the Soviet army. Most of them have undergone retraining and are employed in other areas now, although over 25,000 Ukranians left Latvia after the disintegration of the Soviet Union.

POLES Poles have long been resident in Latvia and are considered one of Latvia's traditional minorities. The number of Poles in the country has barely changed in the past 100 years, including the last 50 years under Soviet occupation.

Two-thirds of the people of Polish origin are now Latvian citizens and most are fluent in Latvian. The Poles have strong cultural traditions and a great interest in maintaining the traditions of Polish culture. In 1995 there were six Polish schools in Latvia and also large Sunday schools and kindergartens.

The Poles are mostly city dwellers concentrated in Riga and Daugavpils.

LITHUANIANS As of 1995, Lithuanians made up 1.42% of Latvia's population, of which the largest concentration is found in the towns of Saldus, Bauska, and Liepaja. A high percentage of Lithuanians are engaged in farming and most have integrated into Latvia. More than half speak Latvian, and there is a high rate of intermarriage.

GERMANS Germans in Latvia occupy a special place among the ethnic minority groups, given that settlers of German descent have lived in the Baltic territories since the 13th century. Over the centuries they have continued to hold the upper levels of authority in the country.

The Germanic influence on Latvian culture remained very strong until Latvia gained its independence in 1918. At that time many Germans left Latvia, unable to reconcile themselves to losing their former privileges and social status. By 1935, the German population had dropped to half of what it had been at the turn of the century. Since 1959, the number of resident Germans has increased, mainly due to Germans moving to Latvia from Russia. Presently, 25.7% of Latvia's Germans are citizens of Latvia.

History is a vital part of the education of Latvia's young generations. Within most schools the various nations that make up the population work and play together.

THE CHANGING SOCIAL STRUCTURE

Until the 19th century, the main occupation in Latvia was agriculture. Most Latvians lived in the countryside as peasants, and there were no class distinctions, as everyone lived off the land and from the labor of their own hands. Those who lived in the towns and cities were small tradesmen, craftsmen, and artisans. The land-owners or barons, who were mostly German, held all the power in local municipalities, and even the local clergymen were controlled by them.

With the coming of the first National Awakening in the second part of the 19th century, Latvians became teachers and ministers and moved into positions of power and responsibility. Some rural Latvians moved to the cities and became involved in trade as owners of businesses and of property. With the development of factories at the end of the 19th century, an industrial working class of Latvians also developed in the cities.

During the period of Soviet occupation, society was dominated by the Communist Party, and leadership shifted to the Russian governing class, while the Latvian population moved back to a lower level in the social structure.

SOCIAL CLASSES

During the years of independence from 1918–1941, the typical social classes of a democratic society evolved—farmers, farm laborers, and small tradesmen in the countryside, and entrepreneurs and workers, along with artists, writers, actors, intellectuals, and bureaucrats in the cities. After regaining independence, Latvians are slowly moving into all levels of society again, although the economic sphere continues to be dominated by Russians through the remnants of the former Communist regime.

The entrepreneurial class is the most powerful, followed by the bureaucrats. However, the top layer of society continues to be very fragile, as the turnover of political elites has been very high. Farmers are in the most difficult situation. The break-up of the collective farms and movement back to small family farms has presented many difficulties—a lack of farming skills and farming equipment, soil that has been depleted over decades, a lack of farm buildings, and the total lack of infrastructure.

Above: **Life on small family farms is hard work. The whole family helps out at harvest time.**

Opposite: **There is evidence today on Latvia's streets of the progress Latvian nationals have made into the higher echelons of society.**

Above: **The basic design of the national dress is the same from region to region, but the color and ornamentation varies, identifying the wearer's home.**

Right: **A weaver creating traditional fabric at a folk museum outside Riga.**

Far right: **A monument to the first army commander, Oskars Kalpaks.**

TRADITIONAL FINERY

Historically, one of the most conspicuous examples of Latvian national identity was the production of fabrics and garments. Fabric was woven in every peasant homestead. During the feudal era, Latvians were forced to wear national dress and forbidden to wear fashionable clothes. The national dress was supposed to be evidence of the wearer's membership in the lower class. Nevertheless, the bright and varied colors of traditional garments livened up the bleak dreariness of their daily lives.

The classic traditional Latvian folk dress dates back to very early times and making it is a living art practiced to this day. The design, choice of fabrics, and ornamentation used has remained unchanged over the centuries, and the style of the dress has been preserved from generation to generation.

FAMOUS LATVIAN PEOPLE

KRISJANIS VALDEMARS (1825–1891)

Krisjanis Valdemars was the leader of the first National Awakening movement. He became one of the first Latvians to attempt a study of the Latvian language and Latvian history. Valdemars published poems and was one of those responsible for publishing the first newspaper in Latvian from St. Petersburg. Valdemars encouraged Latvians to take pride in their language and history. He urged the peasants to buy land and thus gain financial independence, and he advised coastal inhabitants to engage in shipping.

OSKARS KALPAKS (1882–1919)

Oskars Kalpaks began his military career in Russia. After he returned to Latvia, he enlisted in the Latvian army and became the first high commander in 1919. Under his leadership, the Latvian army succeeded in pushing out the Bolsheviks from eastern Latvia during the fight for national liberation between 1917 and 1920. Shortly after this, Kalpaks's forces ousted the German Home Guard Army from western Latvia. Kalpaks is considered a hero by Latvians, as he helped to achieve independence for his country against the Bolshevik and German troops, despite their vast numerical superiority.

KRISJANIS BARONS (1835–1923) Krisjanis Barons devoted 37 years of his life to collecting and systematizing *dainas* ("DAI-nas")—the folk songs of Latvia. Altogether he rescued over 35,000 songs from oblivion, and his extensive research has provided a wealth of information in the fields of folklore, mythology, linguistics, religion, and ancient history.

Barons enrolled in the University of Tartu to study mathematics and astronomy. While there he was active in the Tartu University Latvian Students Club, which was founded and led by Krisjanis Valdemars. From 1860 to 1893, Barons lived in Russia and began his writing career with plays and poetry. He was one of the founders of the first Latvian newspaper and eventually became its editor.

After the newspaper was shut down by the authorities, Barons completed the requirements for his tutoring license and worked as a tutor in Russia. He returned to Latvia in 1893 and began his lifelong work of collecting *dainas*.

LATVIA'S FIRST PRIME MINISTER

Karlis Ulmanis (1877–1942) was Latvia's first prime minister and the last president before the Soviet occupation in 1940. The youngest of three brothers, he was born and raised on a farm and took up agricultural studies in Switzerland and East Prussia, becoming very active in advocating modern farming techniques in Latvia. From 1907 to 1909, he attended school in the United States, graduating from the University of Nebraska.

Returning to Latvia, Ulmanis founded the Latvian Farmers Union, with himself as party leader. It was one of the first organizations to voice the idea of an independent Latvia. It finally got the chance to put theory into action in 1918 when representatives of various organizations and parties formed the National Council after World War I. The Council proclaimed a sovereign Latvian state and appointed Karlis Ulmanis prime minister.

However, because of continuous political instability—each new government lasted an average of only 10 months—there was serious dissatisfaction among a vast sector of the population. In 1934 Ulmanis suspended the constitution and dismissed the *Saeima*, suspending all political parties and concentrating all power in the hands of the cabinet, headed by himself. The economic policy that Ulmanis then put in place had much in common with that of the "New Deal" in the United States, resulting in considerable progress in agriculture, successful development of industry, stable government spending, and a relatively high standard of living for the population.

Tragically, with the occupation of Latvia by the Soviet Union, Ulmanis was deported to Siberia where he died in a prison camp in 1942. His name will be closely tied forever with Latvia's first real period of independence, as he was one of the major forces in achieving democracy and an independent Latvia.

After the Red Army took Riga in January 1919, the Ulmanis government moved to Liepaja, where it was protected by a British naval squadron. But the Germans still occupied Liepaja and intended to take control of the country. This caused a conflict with Ulmanis' government, and the British forced the Germans to retreat. During this time the Red Army, under attack by Estonians, had withdrawn from Latvia.

LIFESTYLE

THE SOUL OF THE LATVIAN is tied to the care of the land and the soil. A Latvian proverb illustrates this feeling perfectly: "He who cares for the land will be fed by the land." This attachment to the soil is evident in much of Latvian tradition, as well as in their literature, painting, music, and sculpture.

The make-up of the extended Latvian family is similar to that in other Western countries—father, mother, children, grandparents, aunts, and uncles—and family ties are usually strong. Two children is considered to be the ideal, and they are usually born and brought up in the family home where they are taught to assume the roles that they will play later in life.

Women have the same rights as men in law since Latvia regained its independence. However, much remains to be done for true equality to emerge, as women are not proportionally represented in politics—very few women are nominated and even fewer are elected.

Opposite: **Latvian children of today are growing up in a country with hope for a bright future.**

Left: **Special occasions, such as festivals and birthdays, warrant a large family gathering in Latvia.**

LATVIAN WOMEN

Women comprise the majority of the population of Latvia. In 1994 women accounted for 54% of the urban population and 52% of the rural population. They also made up 52% of the workforce. Almost one-third of all working women are employed in the education and health services—the lower paid professions.

Women are entitled to maternity leave two months before and two months after childbirth, but if they choose, they are entitled to extend their maternity leave until their child is 3 years old, receiving benefits from the government of up to 40% of the minimum wage. Life expectancy for women is longer than that of men. In 1993 life expectancy was 73.8 years for females and 61.6 years for males.

In more traditional Latvian society, men continue to play a dominant role. The majority of public officials and leaders are men, although more and more women are assuming managerial positions. Men also continue to be regarded as the head of the family.

THE OLDER GENERATIONS

Older people still have an important role in passing on traditions to the next generation, as they are usually the guardians of customs and beliefs and the holders of knowledge and wisdom. Unfortunately, many elderly people live below the poverty line, and during the transition period after regaining independence, the Latvian government has been unable to improve this situation by increasing pensions. The average old-age pension in 1995 was only about 35% of the average wage. As a result, elderly people often become dependent on their children to maintain their standard of living. This is unlikely to get better soon, as approximately 25% of the population of Latvia is already of retirement age.

For every 100 Latvian tax-payers, there are 87 pensioners. This results in low pensions and pushes the burden of their well-being onto the younger generations within the family unit.

URBAN AND RURAL LIVING

The majority of Latvians living in urban areas still live in below-standard housing, due to the construction and ownership of all accommodation by the state during Soviet rule. The apartments built during this period were of very poor quality and received limited maintenance over the 50-year period. Apartments had only one or two rooms, a small kitchen, and a bathroom that was often shared with other families. Houses built before the Soviet occupation may have been of better quality, but many have not been maintained properly and have deteriorated beyond repair.

With the regaining of independence and reinstatement of private ownership of property, there is extensive renovation being carried out on older private homes, apartments, farms, and public buildings, as well as the construction of new ones. Some people own their apartments, which they have been able to buy in new, privately-owned buildings.

Above: **A small self-sufficient family farm on the outskirts of Riga.**

Right: **During the Soviet period, each citizen was officially allocated only six square yards (five square meters) of living space. The large majority of city dwellers still live in relatively small apartments.**

Far right: **There is considerable conflict between those living in rural areas and those living in towns and cities as to how much support agriculture should receive from the government.**

SELF-SUFFICIENCY

During the Soviet period, the urban garden was often a necessity to supplement the meager food supplies with basics such as potatoes, onions, and cabbage, and it continues to play the same role to some extent. However, spiritually, the garden is to the city dweller what the cottage is to the North American—a place to relax, to sit in the sun, and to get out of close living quarters in the city.

In the countryside, the collective farm system that existed during the Soviet era is gradually disappearing, although most country people continue to live in Soviet-era central housing complexes, which are located well away from the fields. Many families are now returning to rejuvenated single-family farms, reconstructing the farm buildings and learning basic farming methods, as a high percentage of these small farms still lack electricity, farm machinery, and proper facilities for the farm animals.

Agriculture was traditionally the mainstay of the Latvian economy, and there are many people who say that agriculture should still be the main thrust of the government's economic policy today. This belief, however, isn't shared by those living in urban areas.

NEW BIRTH

For a Latvian family, the arrival of a newborn child is a time for much celebration and the beginning of a series of personal festivals which will continue to mark the progress through life.

The first of these, the name-giving ceremony, is held on the ninth day after the child's birth and usually lasts for two days. Godparents are chosen for the newborn—only those of unblemished character will do—and it is they who often choose the name for the child. Traditionally, the name was announced during a formal ceremony in which the godparents promise to care for the child in the event the parents die. The newly-named child is then introduced to everyone present and welcomed as a full-fledged member of the family. For the rest of their lives, Latvians continue to celebrate their name day (as well as their birthday) with great feasting. On the date when one's name is celebrated, it is customary to stay home and prepare to welcome guests.

MARRIAGE

Another major event is the wedding, which usually begins with a formal proposal of marriage. Traditionally, this was done through intermediaries speaking to the mother of the bride-to-be and then to her father and brothers. Once the proposal was accepted, a party was held at the bride's house, which often lasted right through the night.

Today, the modern wedding ceremony often takes place in a church where the bride is married in traditional white and attended by bridesmaids. Wedding celebrations often last for three days—although sometimes they can carry on for over a week!

The singing of special songs is an important part of the wedding ritual. After the church ceremonies, a feast is held during which the newlywed couple are initiated as married people. The bride's coronet is replaced with a headdress commonly worn by married women, and the bridegroom is offered a hat appropriate to married men. A shawl is then placed over the shoulders of the couple and the guests sing them a song of welcome to married life.

In times of economic difficulty, the autumn months were a popular time to get married, when food was plentiful.

A TRADITIONAL LATVIAN WEDDING

The festivities of a traditional Latvian wedding begin when representatives of the bridegroom journey to the house of the bride to bring her to the groom's house for the ceremony. The bride—dressed in her finest clothes—says goodbye to all those she has lived with at her parents house, giving them small gifts. Then she leaves with her escort to travel to the groom's house. Once she is there, a formal ceremony is held in which vows and rings are exchanged and the bride's coronet, which symbolizes her maidenhood, is replaced by a headscarf, worn by all married women. After this, a special meal is prepared for everyone to enjoy.

Right: **Nurses preparing for a clinic at a private hospital in Riga.**

Below: **A freshly-baked loaf of bread is offered to the new couple as a symbol of their new unity.**

HEALTH

The recent long years spent under Soviet dominance have resulted in poor living conditions in Latvia and the neglect of health. The birth rate is low and continues to fall, and the death rate—especially infant mortality—is high and continues to rise. Overall life expectancy is 69.1 years, compared to 79 years in neighboring Sweden.

Latvia is supposed to have a state-supported health plan for all inhabitants, but a large proportion of medical costs are currently paid by patients themselves, as the health system, like all other social systems, is currently in a period of transition, and government financial resources are still inadequate. This often means that cancer and other illnesses are diagnosed late, thereby increasing the cost of treatment and reducing the chances of recovery. Diseases that can be linked to poor social conditions, such as sexually transmitted diseases, continue to increase.

Health education is limited, and so those responsible for paying their own medical costs chose other necessities for the family over their own well-being. The number of private hospitals is growing, pushing the waiting lists at state-run institutions to their limit.

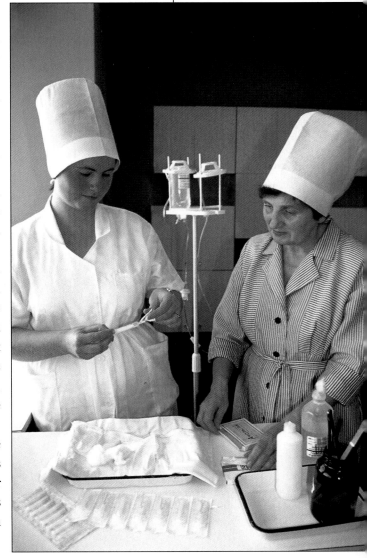

EDUCATION

Latvian children are required to attend school to the age of 15, although preschool attendance is voluntary as not all schools provide kindergartens. In 1995 about 90% of all Latvian students completed basic education (grades 1 to 9), 38% completed secondary education, and 72% of these enrolled in institutions of higher education.

The first law establishing compulsory education for all children was passed in 1919, and education was free. The language of instruction was the language spoken in the family. The compulsory foreign language was at first German, although it was later replaced by English.

Kindergarten children doing their morning exercise routine.

A BROADER CURRICULUM

After World War II, during the period of Soviet occupation, the Latvian school system was Sovietized, and the curriculum was changed according to socialist political theories. The teaching of Latvian language and history diminished, and the number of Russian schools increased. Riga Medical Institute was established in 1950 and a Civil Aviation Engineering Institute was founded in 1960. The general structure of these educational institutions has been retained now that Latvia has regained its independence. Latvian history and literature is taught without "political revisions," and Latvian has become the main language of instruction.

The teaching process was also changed with the regaining of independence, moving away from central control of all subjects taught, to more autonomy within each school. Within guidelines established by the state, schools may vary their curriculum and choose their own teaching methods. The students are taught and encouraged to seek greater personal initiative, independence, and responsibility.

Young Latvian children enjoying dressing up for their drama class.

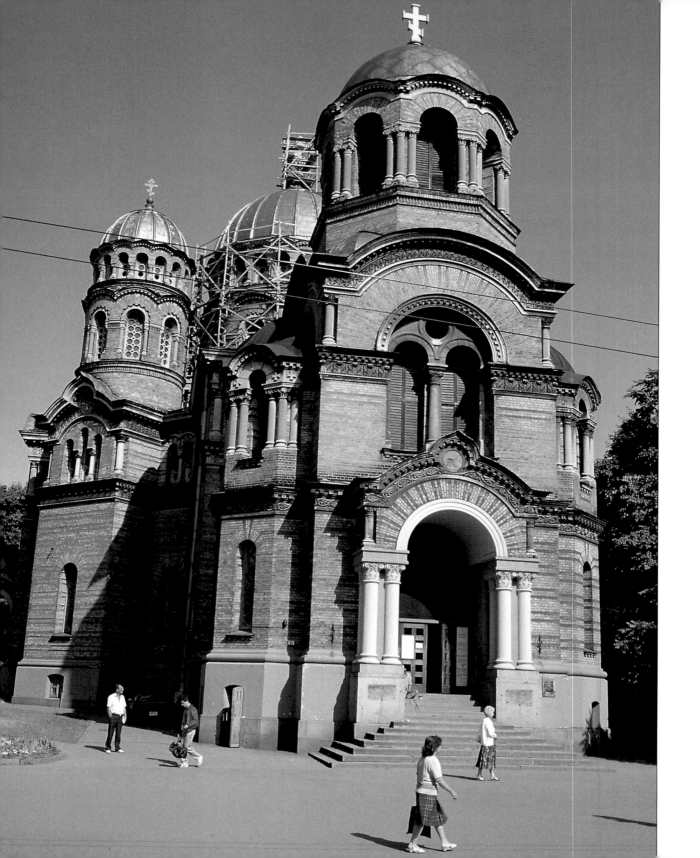

RELIGION

MANY OF LATVIA'S RELIGIOUS BELIEFS AND TRADITIONS originated in ancient times and were passed down through the generations, partly to appease supernatural forces and increase the fertility of the land, and in part to improve personal welfare and commemorate joyous and tragic events.

Worshippers of Latvia's ancient religions gathered at such traditional places as "holy" hills and lakes as well as groves of oak or lime trees. All of creation was viewed as a harmonious entity, to be respected and honored. There were some 5,000 original gods, but only three were worshipped as divine beings—Dievs, Mara, and Laima. Worship of these deities goes back a long way. Over time these old beliefs have been mixed with Christian beliefs, and the original traditions are not always obvious, but there is extensive use of the symbols as design elements in textiles, metals, pottery, and wood.

Opposite: **Jesus Christ Birth Cathedral in Riga. Christianity came to Latvia in the 13th century.**

Left: **Schoolchildren and their teacher sing an ancient religious folk song.**

69

CHRISTIANITY

Christianity was introduced to Latvia in the early 1200s by German monks and Crusaders of the Teutonic Order. Originally, services were held in Latin, and so they were not understood by the Latvians, causing the new religion to spread slowly. It was accepted on the surface, but the familiar traditions and ways held for centuries were continued in secret. Latvians' adherence to their own religious ways was tied closely to the need for continuing resistance against the conquering foreigners.

Right: **Latvia has many fine churches, many of which date back centuries and are wonderful examples of the architecture of various periods.**

LATVIAN CHURCHES

Among the most well-known and finest examples of Latvian church architecture is the Riga Dome Cathedral, known as Rigas Doms. Started in 1211 by Bishop Alberts, the original building was in the Romanesque style with round arches, many of which survive to this day. It was added to in the Gothic style during the next two centuries—the pointed arches built next to the round ones and new structures, such as side chapels and a west transept, were constructed. In the 18th century more additions were made in the Baroque style, and in the 20th century a new entrance hall was built. The cathedral also contains magnificent stained glass windows depicting themes from the Bible and the history of Riga.

CATHOLICISM

The spread of Christianity was tied to the strengthening of German rule in Livonia and the creation of the dominating ruling classes.

The Catholic faith was introduced into Latvia in 1186 when Meinhard, a German monk, became the first bishop. He built a wooden church in which to begin his missionary work, but he met with almost no success at first. His successor, Berthold of Hanover, was appointed bishop of Livonia, but his violent treatment of pagans was his downfall, and he was killed in 1198.

It was not until the arrival of Bishop Alberts of Bushoevden, who succeeded Berthold as bishop, nearly 20 years after Meinhard arrived, that the real conversion of the Latvians to Christianity began. This may have been in part due to his entourage of 23 ships of armed crusaders! Alberts also secured an alliance with King Valdemar of Denmark, who landed in Tallinn with an army in 1219.

The Jesuits attempted to continue the spread of Catholicism after the Bishopric ceased to exist in 1563, but with the spread of the Reformation into Latvia soon after, the Catholic Church quickly lost its influence over most of Latvia, except in the eastern Latgale region.

THE PROTESTANT REFORMATION

The Protestant Reformation started in Riga in 1521 and soon spread throughout Livonia. Lutheranism—the movement adhering to the doctrine of Martin Luther, the leader of the Protestant Reformation in Germany—in particular was further consolidated under 17th century Swedish domination. The clergy wielded comprehensive influence and power over all aspects of daily life, particularly during the feudal period. Permission was necessary for all important acts of one's life, such as the choice of a husband or wife, the date for the marriage, the choice of names for children at baptism, or even permission to attend school.

A Lutheran church in Latvia. The number of Lutheran church members fell from over one million in 1935 before the Soviet invasion to just 350,000 in 1969.

RELIGIOUS FREEDOM

By the time the Republic of Latvia was established in 1918, there were three principal religious denominations in the country—Lutheran, Roman Catholic, and Russian Orthodox.

The church was separated from the state and offences against an individual's beliefs were forbidden by law. During the years of Soviet occupation, religious freedom for all faiths was suppressed. There was large-scale deportation of clergy, and church property was seized by the state. Some churches were turned into concert halls, museums, warehouses, movie theaters, and meeting halls, while others were burned or left to ruin. Membership in all congregations fell dramatically, although the Catholic Church lost fewer members than the Lutherans.

With the regaining of independence in 1991, religious life returned and is flourishing. Religious freedom has been reinstated, and the rights of religious organizations are guaranteed by law. Congregations have regained use of their former properties, and churches are being restored.

Two woman light candles in a Russian Orthodox church in Riga.

LANGUAGE

LATVIAN HAS CONSTITUTIONAL STATUS as the official language of Latvia and is used in all spheres of activity, although any other language may be used in government meetings by agreement. Latvian is also the dominant language of the mass media, although newspapers, broadcasts, and films are also produced in Russian, English, and Swedish.

The Latvian language comes from an ancient Indo-European language that was spoken at about the same time as ancient Greek, Latin, and Sanskrit. Over the centuries, it has been influenced by other languages with which the ancient Latvians came into contact, especially Livonian (now nearly extinct) and Old Russian, which added words related to the church and the law courts.

Two men—Juris Alunans (1832–1864) and Atis Kronvalds (1837–1875)—made the greatest contributions to the development of a close unity between the literary language and the standard spoken idiom.

Opposite: **Following independence from the Soviet Union, Latvian is the predominant language used in all spheres of society.**

Left: **Children in a Latvian language class at a school in Riga.**

HISTORICAL DEVELOPMENT

In contrast to the language of neighboring Lithuania, Latvian has undergone extensive changes over the last few centuries. The largest addition to the Latvian vocabulary came during the Middle Ages from Middle Low German, which added words in the fields of crafts, fashion, and agriculture. Through trade, wars, and invasions, Latvian has been exposed to the influence of many other languages and cultures, including Finnish, Polish, and French.

Until the 19th century, the development of Latvian language and literature was mainly in the hands of German clergymen. Many of them learned and understood the Latvian peasant language and attempted to keep the influence of their native German on Latvian writing to a reasonable level. As a result, no real separation ever developed between the literary language and popular speech.

The most significant period of development for modern Latvian as it is spoken and written today started early in the 20th century. For the first time, Latvian became the principal language of Latvia, although during the long period of occupation, both Latvian and Russian were considered to be official languages and the use of Latvian was discouraged.

LANGUAGE IN LITERATURE

The 19th century was an important period for the development of both the Latvian written and spoken language. It saw the rise of Latvian national literature, which was the first conscious effort of the Latvians themselves to care for their language. Words were coined for the new notions of Western civilization, a necessary process when a peasant idiom is developing into a cultural language.

The development of Latvian was further strengthened through new literary works—especially those of Janis Rainis, who used his numerous translations of Western European classics to help create new means of expression for his poetry, using words that eventually became part of the language.

Rainis's works were famed for their assertion of national freedom and social consciousness. He was banished from Latvia in 1897 because of strict Russian censorship laws, but returned in 1903 to take part in the unsuccessful revolution of 1905. He then left for Switzerland and did not return again until 1920 after Latvia's first independence had been secured. On his return he was elected to the *Saeima* as minister of education and director of the National Theater.

Rainis translated many international literary works, including Goethe's *Faust* and works by Schiller, Shakespeare, Heine, and Pushkin. These translations extended the Latvian vocabulary and also introduced the usage of shorter word forms.

Above: **Janis Rainis's real name was Janis Plieksans. He was born in 1865 in Varslavani, Latvia.**

Opposite: **A Russian conversing with a Latvian. Each nationality speaks at least a little of the other's language.**

This Riga library is well stocked with books in Latvian, Russian, and German in order to provide a service to most of the population.

MODERNIZING LATVIAN

After the country gained independence in 1918, new needs arose for its development into an republic with its own identity. Latvian terminology needed to be developed for the law courts, the administrative system, and for the newly-established university, art academy, and music conservatory. Official Latvian place names were also needed to replace the old Czarist Russian ones.

Present-day standard written Latvian uses a 33-letter alphabet, based on Latin origins. Modern Latvian is expressive and versatile, and is suited for poetry and literature as well as for sophisticated scientific texts.

Presently, 55% of Latvia's population are native speakers of Latvian, and it is spoken by approximately 1.5 million people, although Russian continues to be more commonly heard on the streets of Riga. Latvian is spoken as a first language by minority populations in Russia, the United States, Canada, Europe, Australia, and South America.

THE ROLE OF THE MEDIA

The media is an important factor that affects the tone and usage of the two principal languages in Latvia. Currently, approximately 100 periodicals are published in Latvia, of which some 60 newspapers and magazines are published in Riga. Newspaper circulation figures are fairly small, and the readerships are concentrated around the main cities.

The newspaper *Diena*, the official organ of the Latvian government, publishes in both Latvian, with a daily circulation of around 70,000, and Russian, with a daily circulation of about 16,000. *Neatkariga Rita Avize* has a circulation of about 50,000 and is published only in Latvian.

Diena and *Neatkariga Rita Avize* are the most influential daily newspapers.

LATVIAN GRAMMAR

The earliest texts in Latvian appeared in the 16th century, and the first grammar was developed two centuries later. Janis Endzelins, the most noted Latvian philologist, laid the foundation of modern Latvian grammar and vocabulary through his research and the publication of the book "Latvian Grammar," which created new words and clarified others.

Present-day written Latvian uses a macron, a mark placed over vowels to indicate vowel length, and an accent over or under a consonant to indicate the softer pronunciation of a letter. There are three Latvian dialect groups—East (or High), West, and Central.

The use of a macron over some vowels distinguishes Latvian from the languages of Western Europe.

RADIO AND TELEVISION

About 22 radio stations and 34 television studios broadcast regularly in Latvian and/or Russian. *Latvijas Radio* broadcasts in Latvian and Russian, with newscasts in German and English, as well as in the languages of Latvia's ethnic minorities. Russian state radio is received in Latvia, as are programs from the Voice of America and Radio Free Europe.

Latvian state television was established in 1954. An independent channel was established in 1992, with nightly news broadcasts in Latvian and English. Russian state television and a private channel from Moscow also broadcast in Latvia. Limited broadcasts from CNN, the BBC, and German television are available on state television. The nightly news program, *Panorama*, is the most popular program and is essential viewing for many Latvians.

A Latvian film production crew preparing to shoot some scenes in Riga for a national newscast.

ARTS

CULTURE IN LATVIA IS ANCIENT and dates back to the years before the country was invaded and swamped by the heritage of other nations. Latvia lost its cultural identity during the long years of foreign dominance but since independence, the vitality of its arts have reappeared in many different forms.

The arts thrive through drama groups, choirs, ensembles, orchestras, and dance groups. Latvians are immensely proud of their heritage and, especially since independence in 1991, strive to express themselves and their identity through prose, plays, and music.

Latvia is famous for its song festivals, which have been in existence since the 1870s. They are popular events in Latvia, as well as in Latvian immigrant communities throughout the world.

Every five years, local towns and districts hold competitions for choirs, orchestras, and dance groups to select the best for a national festival.

Opposite and left: **Women and children performing.**

LITERATURE

Although Latvian culture is ancient, its literature is relatively new, having only come into its own during the National Awakening of 1850 to 1880. Before this time, any writing about Latvia was done by foreigners, mainly from Germany.

In 1878 the first classic novel in Latvian, *Merenieku Laiki*, was published. It was written by two brothers, Reinis and Matiss Kaudzitis, who spent 20 years writing the novel. In 1888 another classic work, *Lacplesis,* based on Latvian folklore and written by Andrejs Pumpurs, was published. In 1890 a new era in Latvian literature called the *Jauna Strava* (New Current) began. The most prominent writer of this period was Janis Rainis who was born into a well-to-do family. However, after denouncing the Baltic German barons' exploitation of the Latvian peasants, he was imprisoned and then banished from Latvia for 20 years. Rainis's wife, Aspazija (1868–1943), was a well-known poet in her own right, with strong romantic tendencies. Between them they laid the foundation for modern Latvian drama.

Rudolfs Balaumanis (1863–1908) is perhaps Latvia's greatest playwright. The son of a cook and a maid, he made his living running the comic section of a newspaper. Although he is best known for his tragedies, he wrote comedies as well. His characters are set in an everyday environment, and the relentless turmoil they face within themselves forms the plot of his plays.

Karlis Skalbe (1879–1945), who was known as the Latvian Hans Christian Andersen, wrote deeply nationalistic verse and fairy tales. He was the youngest of 10 children and grew up in poverty. He too lived in exile for his anticzarist activities and was one of the first intellectuals to openly discuss the idea of full independence for Latvia.

During the 20th century, Latvian writers could not produce works with a balanced view of the world, as their exposure to life outside their country was restricted. Instead, their works had psychological themes, depicting the neuroses of modern man.

Opposite: **Strong emotion shows in this performance of a Latvian play. Today, Latvians are proud to be able to display their literary and artistic talents freely.**

DRAMA

After Latvia gained independence in 1918, a new period in Latvian literature and drama began, as the literary climate was stimulating, intellectual, and creative. Realism continued to be the popular style for literature as were themes that glorified the past, although love themes also become quite popular.

The best known poet of this period—and also considered Latvia's greatest modern poet—is Aleksandrs Caks. He disregarded rhyme and used daring and unexpected images. Although his choice of topics was considered shocking at the time, his poems of the 1930s stand out as remarkable works of art.

This period came to an end with the occupation of Latvia by the Soviets in the 1940s. Under the Soviet occupation, the sole aim of Latvian literature was to praise Communism and Stalinism, so literary work became dull and mainly took the form of industrial and agricultural narratives. Nevertheless, a number of well-known Latvian writers were able to practice their craft throughout the years of Soviet occupation, even though some of them suffered greatly from persecution. Some of the better known are the novelist Vizma Belsevica and the poet Imants Ziedonis.

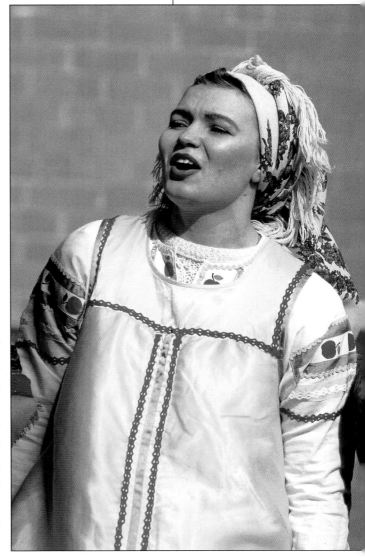

A stage performer taking part in a summer festival.

LITERARY WORK ON THE STAGE

After Stalin's death in 1953, there was a small revival of pre-Soviet Latvian culture, such as folk songs and folk tales, and some literary works of past writers were legalized again. Some of the Latvian writers who had been deported to Siberia were also allowed to return to Latvia and write again.

Since the end of the Soviet occupation, the poet Mara Zalite has adapted the classic Latvian epic, *Lacplesis*, into a rock opera, and the prose of Regina Ezers has begun to deal with the topic of sensitive individuals isolated and destroyed by a totalitarian environment. Vizma Belsevica, a contemporary novelist, was even reportedly considered for the Nobel Prize for Literature in 1992.

A very active literary world has also evolved among the Latvians who fled Latvia at the time of the Soviet takeover and settled in various parts of the Western world. Some of the more famous names include the essayist and novelist Zenta Maurina, who settled in Germany and who became as well known there as she is among the Latvians, and a whole new generation of Latvian poets who developed in exile in New York and are consequently referred to as the "Hell's Kitchen" school of poets.

Although he now lives in Sweden, Andrejs Eglitis is known for his patriotic poetry, which describes the longings for the freedom of Latvia. His poem, *O God, Thy Land is Aflame*, has been set to music and is considered an important reflection on Latvia's struggle for survival and freedom.

MUSIC

Music as long been a part of Latvian cultural life in both formal settings, such as opera houses and theaters, and informal ones, such as the family home or local inn. The enormous variety of musical styles reflects the influences on Latvia's culture from other countries. Latvian folk songs, *dainas*, make up the largest and most important part of the music culture of the country. As many as 400,000 published *dainas* exist, as well as over one million that have never been published or recorded formally. These songs are sung at special occasions, such as weddings, birthdays, and festivals, accompanied by traditional instruments.

The most popular Baltic folk instrument is the *kokle* ("KO-kle"), a stringed instrument that has been played since the 13th century.

OPERA AND BALLET

After Stalin's death in 1953, there was a period of revival of pre-Soviet Latvian culture. Some Latvian writers and composers, who had been deported to Siberia, were allowed to return to Latvia and work again.

The Latvian National Opera, renamed the "Opera and Ballet Theater" under Soviet rule, was opened in 1919 and became a representative art institution of the country. It received substantial government support, which allowed it to keep admission fees low and attract many ordinary people to attend. Visits to the opera remained a popular activity for Latvians, particularly during times of oppression and unrest under the dominant Soviet and German rule.

The activities of the opera company included opera performances, symphonic concerts, and solo concerts by leading musicians. The National Opera also played an important role in promoting the works of Latvian composers. A number of Latvian operas were composed and performed between 1920 and 1940. Even during the Soviet occupation, the National Opera continued to perform classical Russian and standard Western repertoire.

Since independence in 1991, the National Opera building has received a major face-lift, restoring the original facilities to their former grandeur and adding new ones. Latvian National Opera performances continue to attract major guest performers from Europe and elsewhere, and opening nights are gala social events. Currently, the best known contemporary Latvian opera singer is the tenor, Inguss Petersons.

The ballet company of the National Opera began its work in 1919, with the first performance taking place in 1922. From 1922 to 1944, the National Opera ballet produced 28 one-act and 23 longer ballets, with a total number of 1,536 performances. Soloists performed as guest artists in Europe and elsewhere, and the whole company appeared in guest performances in Sweden and Poland.

THEATER

Professional theater also emerged in Latvia during the National Awakening in the second half of the 19th century with the production of the first play in Latvian, written by Alexander Johann Stender. The first performance took place in Riga in 1868. Latvian professional theater dates from 1886, when the Latvian Society in Riga provided space and funding in order to support professional actors, thus laying the foundation for the National Theater of Latvia in Riga, which continues to be one of the foremost theaters in Latvia to this day.

A second theater was founded in Latvia in 1902—*Jaunais Rigas Teatris*—and the reputation of this theater was established with the production of the historical-symbolical plays by Janis Rainis. The set designs were by Janis Kuga, whose scenery and costumes enjoyed wide popularity.

The National Theater of Latvia has recently undergone extensive renovations as this exquisite wall decoration shows.

FOLK SONGS

Music as a cultural expression represents most accurately the Latvian character, as it has been very important in the formation and maintenance of national feelings over the centuries. Folk songs constitute by far the most original and extensive part of Latvian musical tradition.

Latvian folk songs have been passed on from ancient times by direct and verbal communication from one generation to the next. They began to be collected in written form in the 19th century, and this continues to the present day.

The famous Latvian musicologist Krisjanis Barons spent 37 years classifying the texts of *dainas*, collecting over 218,000 songs, of which about 35,800 were original. The total number of collected songs is now so vast that they outnumber the population of the country by two to one!

Latvian folk melodies have influenced the compositions of many Latvian composers of classical music. Pauls Dambis is known for his arrangements of Latvian folk melodies, and Imants Kalnins is a well-known composer. The most famous and prolific Latvian musician is the conductor Mariss Jansons, who conducts many of Europe's best-known orchestras.

DAINAS

The dominant subject of Latvian folk songs is the material and spiritual life of the people. The words deal with the cycle of human life, from the cradle to the grave, and the songs are arranged this way in the published collections. The first volume contains cradle songs and the second volume love songs, while the third volume has songs about marriage and married life. The fourth volume is on work and everyday life.

A *daina* can be philosophical, humorous, joyful, sarcastic, gentle, instructive, comic, or witty, but actually has very little direct connection with history. Proper names are used to refer only to mythological characters and to those found in the ancient religions. Most *dainas* are composed of four-line verses that are divided in two—the first two lines ask a question, while the last two give the answer.

SONGS FOR CELEBRATION

Melodies for these songs can be either recitative in style—sung in a group with a lead singer and a responding choir—or solo songs, sung solo or in a group. Recitative songs do not have a regular text, as the words are improvised according to the requirements of the subject matter and conditions under which the singing takes place. They are sung to mark the celebration of the seasons or the major events of one's life—birth, christening, marriage, funerals—or as work songs telling about plowing, threshing, or herding. The solo song-texts deal with romance, the beauty of nature, or the sorrows of children and orphans.

A female choir taking part in a local arts and culture festival competition.

FOLK SONG FESTIVALS

Folk song festivals have become an important part of the Latvian culture. The first nationwide Latvian Song Festival took place in 1873 in Riga to foster and advance choral singing. The choir consisted of several thousand singers (the audience totalled four or five times that number), while at the ninth festival in 1938 the chorus consisted of 17,000 singers! From the very first song festival developed the tradition that a nationwide song festival would be held at intervals of four to eight years as an important demonstration of Latvian culture and national unity. In June 1998 the 22nd Song Festival took place in Riga.

To tie in with the folk song festivals, many cultural exhibitions and shows are held throughout the country. This man is crafting traditional toys and trinkets at a museum outside Riga.

LATVIAN SONG FESTIVAL

The program for the Latvian Song Festival has become quite extensive. In addition to the concerts, programs now include arts and crafts exhibitions, folk dance performances, theater, and all kinds of instrumental, vocal, and religious concerts.

The festival may last four to five days or more, and although the main festival takes place in Riga, regional concerts and performances are held throughout Latvia in the weeks before the festival. For the past 50 years, similar song festivals have also been held in many other cities around the world where Latvians have taken refuge.

A dance being performed on the cobbled streets of Riga.

TRADITIONAL ARTS AND CRAFTS

Latvia has retained a distinctive folk art, which has its roots in the ancient past but which continues to be active and vibrant to this day. Over the centuries, traditional art was evident in buildings and furniture, as well as in the clothes and jewelry that were created for the everyday needs of the rural population. Traditionally, many peasants mastered several crafts and produced their own tools, utensils, and simple pieces of furniture. In addition, each parish had its own craftsmen who specialized in a particular trade.

The fundamental character of Latvian ornamental design is geometric and abstract, and these traditional designs are still applied to contemporary decorative and applied arts, most commonly in ceramics, metalwork, woodwork, textiles, and wickerwork. The creation of applied decorative arts continues to be a dominant and widespread activity in today's cultural life in Latvia.

A Latvian folk tapestry depicting dancers in traditional dress.

LEISURE

WITH INCREASING ECONOMIC STABILITY IN LATVIA, activities requiring expensive sports equipment, such as skiing and sailing, are gaining in popularity, and more leisure time is devoted to reading, attending cultural events such as concerts, theater, opera, and other performing arts.

Latvians also love to stroll through their city or town parks, taking evening or Sunday afternoon walks enjoying some gentle exercise with the whole family. Hunting and fishing, hiking, gardening, traditional folk dancing and singing, and craft-making are also popular leisure activities.

Games are an integral part of the traditional culture of Latvians. Traditionally, they are of two types—games with music, where the participants sing along during the game, and games without music, where participants perform certain actions.

Opposite: **A grandmother and child feed the ducks in a town park.**

Left: **Latvia's towns are littered with parks and playgrounds where children can enjoy playing together.**

Above: Some young people like learning traditional lace-making skills.

Opposite: Two young girls in national dress enjoy a break during game-playing at a local festival.

TRADITIONAL GAMES

A traditional game that may be played by children is called *Viens, divi, tris, pedejais paris skiras!* (One, two, three, last couple separate!). Participants form a column, in pairs, except for a single person at the front of the column who does not have a partner. He/she calls out: "*Pedejais paris skiras!*" and on hearing this, the last couple in the column run to the front of the column, while the single player tries to catch one of them before they reach the front of the line. Whoever remains single takes over the shouting until a partner is caught again!

Another popular game that is still played in the countryside, takes place during Easter. A swing is constructed and hung in the farmyard or nearby woods and all the inhabitants take a turn on the swing on Easter morning. Gifts are exchanged—particularly colorful Easter eggs—and unmarried men may be given hand-knitted mitts or colorful woven sashes by unmarried women, as a token of love.

STORYTELLING

Despite centuries of foreign dominance, it was through the oral tradition that Latvians developed their culture and identity and preserved their sense of nationality.

The most popular activity is singing, but folk tales and legends, anecdotes, riddles, proverbs, folk beliefs, and sayings are common, too. The usual subject matter is everyday rural life and social customs and behavior.

RIDDLES

Some 450,000 riddles have been collected by the Latvian Folklore Institute. They are short, usually only two to six words long, and expressed simply and succinctly. Most have only one correct answer. For example—"What always wears a green frock, summer and winter?" is a spruce tree; "What does not have hands, does not have a loom, yet weaves?" is a spider; "What is high above during the day, down below during the night?" is the sun; and "What flies like a bird but is not a bird, stings like a snake but is not a snake?" is a mosquito.

Folk sayings and parables represent collective folk wisdom. Many of the sayings are common to those of other European cultures as they came into Latvia through the church.

A NEW FREEDOM

Since the recent return to independence in Latvia, people have enjoyed a freedom not experienced before. The younger generations had never had contact with cultures of the West before the removal of the Iron Curtain. Today, through the popularity of American and European music, movies, and books Latvians' once restricted leisure activities have broadened. The older generations are relishing a return to their national identity, and apart from spending time discussing the fascinating historical changes they have experienced, many like to catch up with old friends over a game of chess or cards.

Chess playing outside the cafés of Riga is a popular pastime for young and old alike.

SPORTS

Sports are popular in Latvia. Soccer, basketball, volleyball, track and field, wrestling, tennis, ice hockey, orienteering, motor sports, or even beach volleyball all take place, weather permitting, around the country.

Swimming is popular with Latvian youngsters, and there are municipal pools in most big towns and cities. Schools also encourage swimming as part of the physical education curriculum.

Latvia's debut in the Olympics took place in 1924 when 38 athletes joined in the summer games. The most famous early Olympian was the long-distance walker, Janis Dalins, who won the silver medal for the 50-kilometer walk in 1932. In total, since the 1952 Olympic Games, Latvian athletes have won 18 gold, 26 silver, and 14 bronze medals. In 1988 Latvia was invited to rejoin the Olympic organization as an independent nation.

Above: **A national ballroom dancing competition in Riga. Ballroom dancing has become popular in recent years, and Latvians are now appearing in international competitions.**

Left: **Young schoolchildren enjoy a game of water polo in their school pool.**

FESTIVALS

LATVIA HAS MANY DIFFERENT FESTIVALS that celebrate secular and religious traditions and major historical events.

Latvian festivals tend to be seasonal. The festival of Martini takes place at the beginning of November, when the religious festivities begin for Christmas and last until after the New Year. There are various festivities in the springtime, celebrating the equinox and the beginning of the summer. The biggest festival of the year, *Janu Diena*, celebrates the summer solstice and involves singing, dancing, and feasting. Houses are cleaned and foliage is used to make wreaths and garlands.

Traditionally, at the end of the summer there were two more festivals— one in August to anticipate the end of the hot period and another in September to welcome the autumn equinox and remember the souls of the dead.

Opposite: **Pretty Latvian girls celebrating a festival in springtime.**

Left: **Young children covered by flowers and foliage at the biggest festival of the year, *Janu Diena*.**

Enormous bunches of foliage are gathered to create the wonderful wreaths and headdresses worn on *Janu Diena*.

MIDSUMMER MADNESS

Many of the festivals combine ancient beliefs with modern celebration, and nowhere is this more apparent than in Latvia's most popular holiday, *Janu Diena* (Jani's Day). The festival, which celebrates midsummer, begins on the evening of June 23 and continues into the next day. As the festival approaches, songs with a special refrain resound everywhere, awaiting the arrival of Janis, the son of God, who personifies the festival. Janis is pictured as a tall and handsome man, dressed in beautiful clothes and riding a large horse. He wears the traditional adornment of the occasion—a wreath of oak leaves—on his head.

On the evening of June 23, called *Ligo Vakars* or *Janu Vakars* (Jani's Eve), the celebration of the summer solstice takes place. Jani's Eve has retained most of its ancient pre-Christian flavor. This means a whole night of singing, dancing, merriment, and fortune-telling, until the sun comes up the next morning! Special beer is brewed and a special cheese is prepared. After dusk, fires are lit on the hilltops.

WREATHS AND DECORATIONS

June 23 is also considered the best day of the year to gather medicinal herbs. Flowers and greenery are collected to make wreaths of flowers for the women and men—especially men called Janis (the most common men's name)—to wear during the festivities. Everything is decorated with greenery, while mountain ash branches, thistles, and other sharp objects are placed over building entrances to ward off evil spirits.

The following day's activities include old customs believed to enlist the aid of the spirits of the home, field, and forest. They are intended to help provide a good harvest, by shielding crops and livestock from evil.

Janu Diena is a time for feasting as well as celebrating in the fields. This family is enjoying a well-earned feast after a day of festivities in the fresh air.

CHRISTIAN HOLIDAYS

Many Latvian holidays are very similar to those in other Western countries. Latvians celebrate all the main holidays of the Christian world, with the biggest celebrations taking place at Easter and Christmas.

There are echoes in the modern celebrations of ancient festivals that were once celebrated in Latvia at the same time of year before the coming of Christianity. Christmas and Easter are times for reflection and celebration for both Christian and non-Christian families. They are special occasions when the whole family can celebrate together. Latvians always celebrate in style and everyone makes an effort to dress up for the occasion.

Latvians love to dress up and their many festivals give them the opportunity to create wild and wonderful costumes!

A young Latvian child
visits Santa's grotto in a
Riga department store.

CHRISTMAS

Christmas—the Latvian word is *Ziemassvetki*, meaning winter feast—
celebrates not only the birth of Christ on December 25, but also reflects
a direct connection with the ancient winter solstice celebrations held by
Latvians long ago.

Christmas is by far the most festive occasion for Latvians—the return of
light at the winter solstice is heralded by the arrival of the celestial
beings called Dievadeli and the Four Brothers Ziemassvetki, who
represent the four days traditionally allowed for celebration of the
Christmas period.

Typically at this time, houses are decorated with straw and feather
decorations, and with *puzuri* ("PU-zu-ri"), diamond-shaped chandelier
decorations made from straw or twigs. Tables are set high with
generous amounts of different foods, such as pig's snout, bacon rolls,
and boiled brown peas.

THE BUDULU CUSTOM

During the weeks before Christmas, the *budulu* custom is celebrated. Disguised in costumes and accompanied by singing, dancing, and much joviality, people call on their friends and neighbors. The festive masqueraders represent good spirits, whose songs and dances are intended to bring good luck to people and fertility to the fields and livestock. Their dances are characterized by "stomping" steps designed to "stomp out all the weeds from the fields." The procession also drags a Yule log along, to be burned at the last stop. This represents the sun recovering its warmth, as well as consuming the past year's misfortunes.

The sieve man, on the left, is a symbol of fertility, appearing prior to Christmas as part of the *budulu* ("BU-du-lu") custom.

FESTIVAL ACTIVITIES

Fortune-telling is a popular activity during Christmas and New Year celebrations. Molten lead is poured into water where it solidifies into an abstract form. The future is predicted by studying the shape of the shadow cast on a wall by this "sculpture."

Similarly, a common tradition on Easter Sunday in Latvia is for neighbors to gather at a swing hung from a pole between two trees and watch as young people try to swing as high as the tree tops. Swinging high ensures a good harvest during the coming summer. Gifts are also exchanged, particularly colorful Easter eggs.

Schoolchildren collect colorful spring flowers in preparation for the Easter festivities.

Although Latvian history has been fraught with suffering and hardship, today Latvians celebrate their national festivals with great enthusiasm.

HISTORICAL HOLIDAYS

Some of the Latvian holidays also celebrate events which have made deep impressions on Latvia's history and on the lives of its people.

June 14 is the commemoration day of victims of the Communist terror when, on the night of June 13, 1941, the first mass deportations were made by the Soviet powers. Some 15,000 Latvians from all walks of life, including the old, the infirm, children, and babies, were arrested without trial, and without legal justification, were herded into freight trains and transported under guard to Siberia to forced labor camps or *gulags* ("GOO-lags").

November 11, Lacplesa Day, is the Memorial Day of the fight for independence, commemorating all who have fought in defense of Latvia, while May 4 is the proclamation day of the Republic of Latvia, which celebrates the declaration of a free and independent Latvia in 1991.

CALENDAR OF ANCIENT LATVIAN FESTIVALS

Many festivals were celebrated in Latvia years ago marking the changing seasons. Ritual activities took place and special foods were eaten.

Metini (February 18–19)
Celebrated the end of *kekatas* ("CHE-ka-tas")—the carnival activities of Christmas—with sleigh rides and masquerades. Weavers made cloth with their freshly-spun yarns and on the farm young horses were broken in.

Great Day (May 20–23)
Celebrated the day and night of equal length—the spring equinox. The ritual activities included washing before sunrise in running water, hanging swings, and chasing birds. It was the time when the days were longer, and the farmers no longer had to use lights in the evenings.

Usini (April 19–20)
The official beginning of summer, celebrated many centuries ago, when roosters were killed in order to silence them, and their blood was drained into horse troughs. Crosses were painted on doors with the blood and horses were taken to swim before sunrise. The ritual foods were eggs, boiled rooster, and beer. The evening grazing of horses and cattle began, and it was plowing and sowing time for the farmers.

Janu Diena (June 23–24)
The longest day and shortest night—the summer solstice. The activities were similar to those of today—flower wreaths were made, bonfires were lit, and songs were sung. The ritual foods were cheese, bread, pies, meat dishes, and beer. On the farm, haying started.

Apjumibas or Rudenaji (September 23)
The autumn equinox and the beginning of the period of the souls of the dead. Lots of meat was eaten and winter crops were sown.

Martini (November 10)
The end of the celebration of the souls and the beginning of masquerade time, leading up to Christmas. Martini balls, made of peas, beans, potatoes, and hemp, were the festival food.

Jani's Day, or Janu Diena, *is one of the oldest Latvian holidays and is a well-known festival throughout Eastern Europe. Beer is brewed specially for the day, and a cheese called Janu Cheese is made using caraway seeds.*

FOOD

IN ANCIENT LATVIA food was traditionally prepared in one of two main locations—the house where everyone lived, or in a specially-constructed building with an open hearth. In the latter case, the hearth was usually placed as far away from the other farm buildings as possible. Most dishes were prepared in a cast-iron pot, placed on an open fire. Water was carried up from the well and stored in wooden pails.

Basic food staples were homegrown, preserved, and prepared. The basic foods were grains, various kinds of meat, saltwater fish (or preserved fish in some regions), and dairy products. Commonly grown garden vegetables such as potatoes, cabbage, beets, turnips, carrots, peas, and beans were also eaten, as were wild greens—sorrel, nettles, thistle, and goose foot—in the spring and wild berries, wild hazelnuts, and mushrooms in the late summer and fall.

Opposite: **Children enjoying a party feast. Most Western-style treats are available in Latvia today.**

Left: **As the Latvian economy grows, more people can afford to appreciate fine foods. This mural provides a colorful backdrop to a romantic restaurant setting.**

BREAD

Bread was—and still is—a staple food at every meal, baked from rye or barley flour, or for special occasions, from wheat or buckwheat flour. Dough for bread was prepared in a large, elongated wooden trough, approximately four feet (1.2 m) in length, with handles. The bread was baked in special ovens, where the loaf was placed on a flat, wide wooden shovel to be transferred onto the hot coals.

Baking was done in large quantities, usually in large loaves. On special occasions, rolls might also be baked, with butter and/or egg wash added, or with special toppings, such as grated carrots.

Just as in the olden days, bread is an important part of the Latvian diet today.

PORRIDGE AND MEAT

Years ago, porridge was the most commonly served dish and was prepared from pearl barley and other grains. Vegetables, as well as milk, and some meat or lard were added. The content of the porridge or gruel usually depended on what produce was available at a given time of year, or the financial situation of the household.

Meat was consumed sparingly and on special occasions, as most of it was taken to the market to be sold. Only affluent families could afford to eat meat regularly, and in the countryside fresh meat was often only available when an animal was slaughtered, usually in the fall. Every part of the animal was prepared for consumption—the best cuts were usually sold and the secondary cuts prepared for home consumption, including the blood, head, feet, and innards.

Today, workers prepare meat for sausage-making at a factory in Leipaja.

The traditional Latvian diet was heavy in starch and lacking in protein, calcium, and vitamins. Today, fresh fruit and vegetables, as well as different meats, are available in shops and markets.

EXTRA FLAVORS

Ground hemp seed prepared with salt and green onions was used in place of butter. Butter was used only on special occasions, and fresh milk was usually saved for the children, to be added to porridge and gruel, or made into yogurt and cottage cheese. Honey was used as a sweetener—salt and sugar were used with great care as they were often the only food products that had to be bought.

DRINKS

Juice prepared from birch or maple sap was a very popular nonalcoholic drink. It was prepared in the springtime in large quantities so that it could last most of the summer.

Today, ale and beer are sometimes home-brewed from barley with hops added and served at all important occasions, such as harvesting. It is sometimes available at pubs, along with commercially brewed drinks.

MEALS

Latvians usually eat three meals a day. In the olden days, a fourth meal was often added in the afternoon. In those days, the midday meal was usually the main meal of the day—gruel served with lard or fat, and cabbage or sauerkraut. The afternoon extra meal included bread, cottage cheese, buttermilk, and sometimes herring. For supper Latvians ate potatoes with a flour or mushroom gravy, or milk gruel with bread. Each day of the week a particular type of dish was served, and supper on Saturdays as well as the meals on Sundays might also include some special dishes or treats.

In olden times, the whole household ate at the same table, but not at the same time. Today, that tradition has changed and large extended families will share a meal together at a big table.

EAT, DRINK, AND BE MERRY

Today, Latvian's are known for their strong hospitality. Regardless of the economic situation of the host, a guest will be treated to all that the host has. Often the poorest people are the most hospitable and nothing is spared. Latvians like to entertain, and a formal dinner is taken seriously. Like other inhabitants of the northern countries, Latvians like to eat and drink, but they do not drink more than any other European and they usually have drinks together with a meal.

Dishes prepared for a Latvian feast are chosen according to the produce available at a particular time of year, but the central dish of any festive meal is the meat course. Food is most plentiful in the fall when the harvest has been brought in—special breads are baked for the occasion. Oven-baked turnips are served and also carrots, peas, potatoes (cooked and served with fried smoked bacon), onions, and hemp seed, formed into balls. Honey and apples are served for dessert, as well as a rich cake on very special occasions.

FALL FEASTS

Traditionally, special family occasions were usually held in the fall when food was plentiful, and on special feast days such as Martini (November 10), goose or capon were served. For Christmas and New Year's Eve, traditional dishes were smoked pig's snout, braised sauerkraut or cabbage, and blood pudding served with red bilberry preserves, peas, and beans. For special occasions in the spring, eggs were the special dish, as well as jelled veal or pork and milk pudding. For summer festivities, the special dishes were made with dairy products, such as cheeses, served with specially-baked rolls, butter, and *piragi* ("PEE-raa-gi")—crescent-shaped baked buns filled with savory onion and bacon.

Friends enjoy a picnic outdoors during the mild summer months.

These impressive cakes are typical examples of Latvian treats made at Christmastime.

LATVIAN FOOD TODAY

Today, the foods that Latvians eat are very similar to those eaten in many other countries. Breakfast usually consists of coffee, boiled or fried eggs, fried potatoes, rye or white bread, and butter or cottage cheese. Lunch may be a hardy soup with meat, and a meat dish followed by a dessert of fruit compote, bread pudding, or a bread soup with raisins or apples.

A Latvian supper may consist of many different dishes, such as milk soup, pasta, porridge with meat, fried fish, boiled potatoes with pork, or cottage cheese. After supper, the typical Latvian may drink milk, tea, or coffee with bread, butter, jam, or honey.

On Sundays there is usually a more elaborate meal with a special main course, such as meat patties, meat loaf, or cabbage rolls, and desserts like pancakes with jam or a fruit fool are prepared.

HOW TO MAKE A BIRTHDAY KRINGEL

On birthdays and at name ceremonies and name days, a special cake called a *kringel* is prepared. This is a rich bread or coffee cake that is often used as a traditional birthday cake, shaped as a huge pretzel and decorated with candles.

$^1/_2$ to 1 cup sugar
2 tbsps dried yeast
2 cups cream
6 $^1/_2$ cups all-purpose flour
$^1/_2$ lb (0.225 kg) butter
3 egg yolks
grated rind and juice of one lemon
grated rind of one orange
$^1/_2$ tsp Spanish saffron
$^1/_2$ tsp ground cardamom
1 tsp salt
1 $^1/_2$ cups golden raisins
$^1/_2$ cup slivered almonds

Mix 1 tsp sugar and $^1/_4$ cup warm water. Sprinkle yeast on top. Let this mixture stand for 10 minutes until it has bubbled up. In a large bowl combine the cream with the yeast mixture. Add half the flour, mixing well.

Beat the butter with sugar and egg yolks. Add to the dough. Add grated rinds, juice, saffron, cardamom, and salt. Add remaining flour to washed and dried raisins. Mix until the dough is smooth. Then cover and let rise again until doubled in size.

Place the raised dough on a floured board and knead until smooth and elastic. Grease a large cookie pan. Stretch dough into a fat, long strand with tapered ends. Place the dough on the pan and shape into a large pretzel by twisting the ends together.

Smooth and even out the shape all over, making cup-sized holes on both sides of the center. Beat an egg with a bit of water, brush the dough all over, and sprinkle with almonds. Let rise again. Bake in a preheated oven at 350°F (180°C) until golden brown (35–45 minutes). Cool on the pan. Dust with confectioner's sugar and serve on a pretty tray with doilies underneath, with or without candles.

Skaba putra—*consisting of cooked barley groats with buttermilk, yogurt, or milk—and* miestins—*dry pieces of rye bread soaked in water and honey—were popular snacks for hungry Latvian farmers in the early 1900s.*

QUICK NOTES

AREA
25,400 square miles (65,786 square km)

POPULATION
2,490,600 (1996 estimate)

CAPITAL
Riga

OFFICIAL NAME
The Republic of Latvia

OFFICIAL LANGUAGE
Latvian

HIGHEST POINT
Gaizins (1,017 ft / 310 m)

MAJOR LAKE
Lake Rezna

RIVERS
Daugava, Lielupe, Venta, Gauja

MAIN RELIGIONS
Protestant (Lutheran), Roman Catholic, Russian
Orthodox

CLIMATE
Temperate, with mild winters and warm
summers

MAJOR CITIES
Riga, Daugavpils, Liepaja, Jelgava, Ventspils

REGIONS
Zemgale, Kurzeme, Vidzeme, Latgale, Riga

NATIONAL FLAG
Two horizontal stripes of maroon with a white
horizontal stripe through the center. First
adopted as the national emblem in 1917, it was
prohibited during Soviet occupation, but
restored again as the national flag with the
regaining of independence in 1991.

CURRENCY
1 lat = 100 santims
US$1 = 0.6 lat / 60 santims

MAIN EXPORTS
Lumber, agricultural products

MAJOR IMPORTS
Machinery and equipment, textiles and clothing,
chemical products, vehicles, prepared food

POLITICAL LEADERS
Karlis Ulmanis—first prime minister and last
   president before the Soviet occupation
Guntis Ulmanis—president
Vilis Kristopans—prime minister

ANNIVERSARIES
Proclamation Day (May 4)
Memorial Day of the fight for independence
   (November 11)
Proclamation of Independence for the first
   Republic of Latvia (1918) (November 18)

GLOSSARY

āainas ("DAI-nas')
Latvian folk songs.

Dieavadeli
A celestial being representing one of the four days of celebrations at Christmastime.

equinox
The time when the sun crosses the equator, making day and night the same length throughout the world.

gulags ("GOO-lags')
Prison camps in northern Russian and Siberia under the Soviet Communist rule.

Janu Diena
Festival celebrating the summer solstice.

kekatas ("CHE-ka-tas")
Carnival activities enjoyed in ancient Latvia before Christmas.

kokle ("KO-kle")
A stringed instrument dating back to the 13th century played with a pick.

Lutheran
Protestant Churches adhering to the doctrine of Martin Luther, leader of the Protestant Reformation in Germany.

macron
A mark placed over a vowel to indicate that the vowel is long.

Martini balls
Festival food, made of peas, beans, potatoes, and hemp.

piragi ("PEE-raa-gi")
Crescent-shaped baked buns filled with savory onion and bacon.

puzuri ("PU-zu-ri")
Diamond-shaped chandelier decorations made from straw or twigs used at Christmastime.

Reformation
A 16th century religious movement modifying Roman Catholic practice and establishing the Protestant Church.

Saeima
Latvian parliament.

sauerkraut
A dish, originating in Germany, made of finely chopped cabbage pickled in brine.

solstice
A point in time when the sun is at its furthest distance, north or south, from the equator.

Stalinism
The theory and practice of Communism developed by the Russian leader, Joseph Stalin, characterized by Russian nationalism.

Ziemassvetki
The Latvian word for Christmas.

BIBLIOGRAPHY

Dreifelds, June. *Latvia in Transition*. Cambridge, England: Cambridge University Press, 1996.

Haynes, Jim (ed). *Lithuania, Latvia, Estonia: The Baltic Republics (People to People Guides)*. Zephr Press, 1993.

Punga, Inara Astrida, and Hough, William (contributor). *Guide to Latvia*. Chalfont St. Peter, England: Bradt Publications, 1995.

Smith, Graham (ed). *The Baltic States: The National Self-Determination of Estonia, Latvia, and Lithuania*. London, England: St. Martin's Press, 1996.

Von Rauch, Georg, and Onn, Gerald (translator). *The Baltic States: The Years of Independence: Estonia, Latvia, and Lithuania*. London, England: St Martin's Press, 1996.

INDEX

INDEX

INDEX

PICTURE CREDITS